PIANO · VOCAL · GUITAR

REBECCA ST. JAMES
WORSHIP GOD

ISBN 0-634-04661-6

HAL·LEONARD®
CORPORATION
7777 W. BLUEMOUND RD. P.O. BOX 13819 MILWAUKEE, WI 53213

Visit Hal Leonard Online at
www.halleonard.com

LET MY WORDS BE FEW

Words and Music by MATT REDMAN
and BETH REDMAN

Original key: D♭ major. This edition has been transposed up one half-step to be more playable.

SONG OF LOVE

Words and Music by REBECCA ST. JAMES,
MATT BRONLEEWE and JEREMY ASH

Original key: B major. This edition has been transposed down one half-step to be more playable.

BREATHE

Words and Music by
MARIE BARNETT

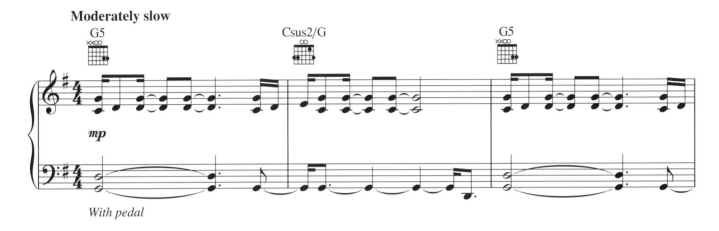

This is ___ the air ___ I breathe, ___

this is ___ the air ___ I breathe, ___

Your ho - ly pres -

Original key: G♭ major. This edition has been transposed up one half-step to be more playable.

GOD OF WONDERS

Words and Music by MARC BYRD
and STEVE HINDALONG

LAMB OF GOD

Words and Music by REBECCA ST. JAMES,
MATT BRONLEEWE and JEREMY ASH

ABOVE ALL

Words and Music by PAUL BALOCHE
and LENNY LeBLANC

BETTER IS ONE DAY

Words and Music by
MATT REDMAN

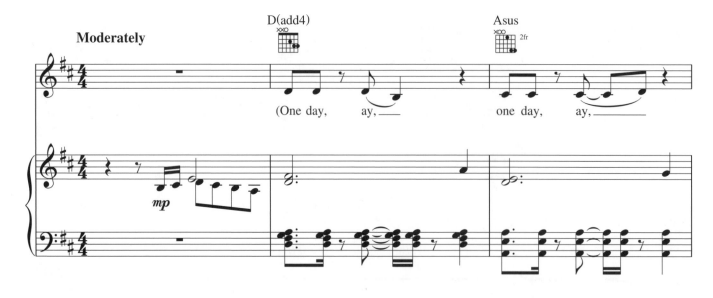

(One day, ay, ___ one day, ay, ___

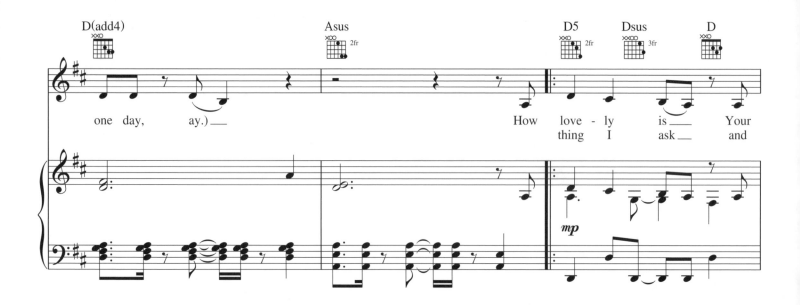

one day, ay.) ___

How love-ly is ___ Your
thing I ask ___ and

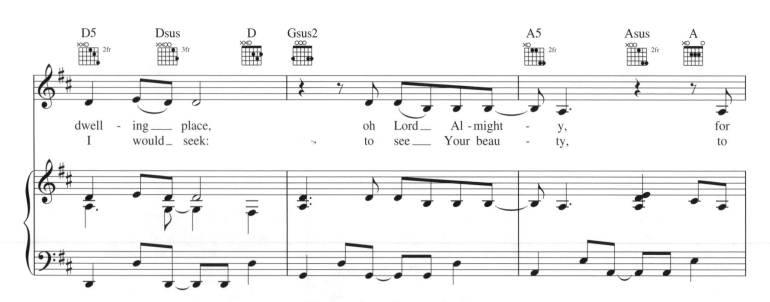

dwell - ing ___ place,   oh Lord ___ Al - might - y,   for
I would ___ seek: to see ___ Your beau - ty,   to

QUIET YOU WITH MY LOVE

Words and Music by REBECCA ST. JAMES
and MATT BRONLEEWE

Come to Me, __ all who are wea - ry, __ and I will give you __ rest. __
Come to Me, __ all who are wea - ry, __ and take My yoke up - on __

__ you. __
__ you. __

Come to Me, __ all who are wea - ry, __ and
Come to Me, __ all who are wea - ry; __ My

Original key: B major. This edition has been transposed up one half-step to be more playable.

MORE THAN THE WATCHMEN

Words and Music by
JEREMY CASELLA

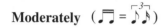

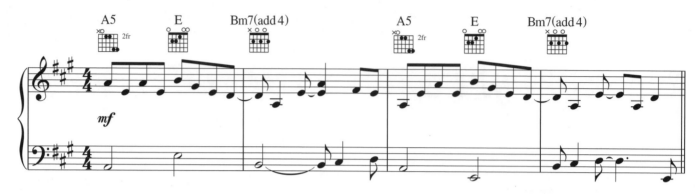

Out of ___ the depths ___ of my ___ de-spair, ___ oh I ___ cry, "Fa-ther hear ___ my ___ voice." ___

___ O-pen Your ears ___ to hear ___ my ___ mer-cy cry. ___

More than the watch - men wait___ for morn - ing, my soul, it waits_ for You.

More than the watch - men wait___ for morn - ing.

- ing.

Vocal solo ad lib.

More than the watch - men wait_ for morn - ing, my soul, it waits_ for You.

52

IT IS WELL

Words by HORATIO G. SPAFFORD
Music by PHILIP P. BLISS

Driving Rock

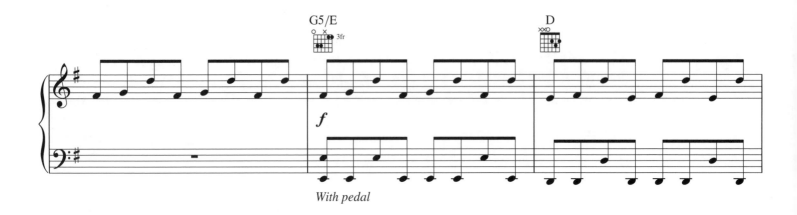

With pedal

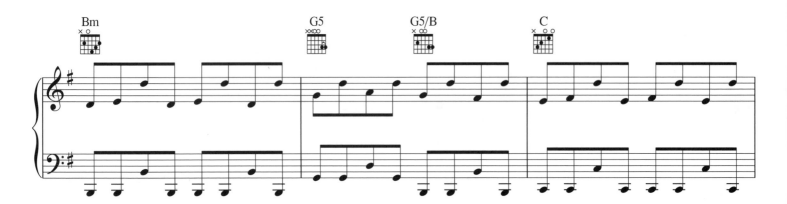

When

dim.

YOU

Words and Music by
REBECCA ST. JAMES

Moderately slow

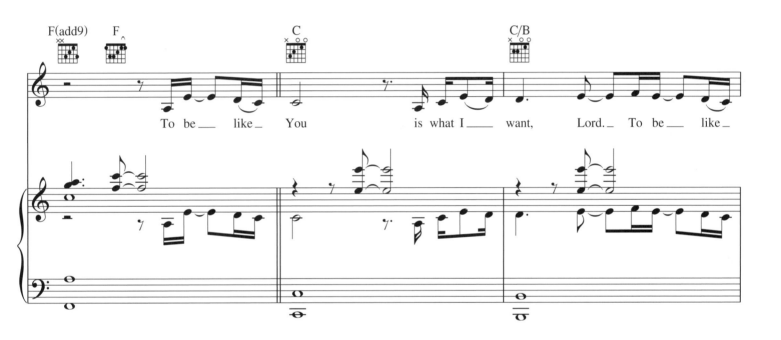

To be ___ like ___ You ___ is what I ___ want, Lord. ___ To be ___ like ___

You ___ is what I ___ ask for. ___ To be like You ___ is what ___ I'm ___

OMEGA
(Remix)

Words and Music by REBECCA ST. JAMES
and TEDD TJORNHOM

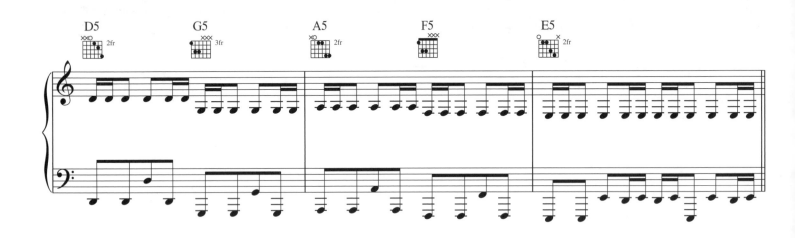

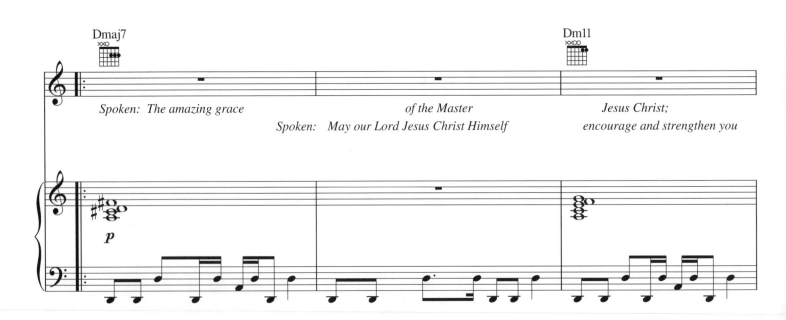

Original key: A♭ minor. This edition has been transposed up one half-step to be more playable.